Robert Adam's COUNTRY HOUSES

Geoffrey Beard

Illustrated by A F Kersting FRPS

John Bartholomew & Son Ltd
Edinburgh, 1981

△ *1 Robert Adam (Tassie medallion) c.1792*

Contents

(Front cover)
Newby Hall, Library, c.1769-70

Introduc

The English patron's enthusiasm for building and embellishing great country houses, especially in the eighteenth century, not only demanded large financial resources, but also provided an opportunity for new decorative styles to evolve and gain acceptance. The architects and craftsmen employed during this period possessed both abundant energy and a wide variety of talents, and they produced schemes of building and decoration that were both diverse and accomplished. These ranged from the classically proportioned columns and porticoes of Palladianism and the exuberant swirling forms of the Rococo to the mannered elegance of the Gothic and Chinese styles. The last half of the century encompassed the ordered symmetry of Neoclassicism. This new mood was given a significant and influential direction by the efforts, in particular, of the architect ROBERT ADAM, born at Kirkcaldy in Scotland on 3 July 1728. The style he championed for his major works was fused into a personal statement that based itself on his early Scottish training — his father William (1689-1748) and his elder brother John (1721-92) were successful mason-architects with a considerable practice — his Grand Tour of Italy, and his extensive studies in Rome, 1754-8.

After being nearly four years in Italy, Robert Adam came to realize that the Romans had invested their buildings and interiors with a freedom of execution denied them by precise theorists and producers of books on antiquity in later years. This freedom, reticulation, expression of taste and concern for symmetry he abstracted carefully. He had been helped to see this freedom not only through his own observation and that of his friends and tutors but by the work of several artists and engravers, such as Charles-Louis Clérisseau and Giovanni Battista Piranesi. He returned to England, filled with ideas, laden with sketches, engravings and works of art, and in 1759 set himself up in London as an architect. His concern was to attract wealthy patrons who needed to build or remodel country houses, and who were keen, through their own travels and observations abroad, to employ someone who could provide a touch of contrived and precise antiquity. Within a year or two of his return — in 1761 — he had made enough of a mark to be appointed by King George III — with his architect rival, William Chambers — as Joint Architect of His Majesty's Works. This achievement brought him an even more active private interest in his work, and building was already in progress at Syon and Kedleston.

(Inside front cover)
Syon House, Entrance Hall, c.1761.

SYON HOUSE, Brentford, London

The Duke of Northumberland

Syon was one of Robert Adam's most important early commissions, and is probably only rivalled in his considerable achievements by the work at Kedleston. In 1762, Sir Hugh Smithson, soon to be created 1st Duke of Northumberland *(pl.2)* turned to Adam to remodel his wife's house, a former nunnery. It has been suggested that the long gallery of the house 'may be the place where the Adam style was actually initiated.' Its Jacobean meagre width *(pl.3)* was a disability the architect overcame by the brilliant use of Corinthian pilasters, in a carefully contrived system of verticals and horizontals. Contrasted by the great heavy majestic Hall of 1761 *(inside front cover)* at Syon the change is remarkable. It shows that despite breaking away gradually over the next few years from heaviness to assured lightness of touch, Adam was already capable of doing so when the occasion demanded. The Syon Gallery stands as testimony to this achievement.

The Drawing Room *(pl.4)* also exemplifies the attention given. It is a complex amalgam of painted roundels by Giovanni Battista Cipriani, red damask walls, ormolu decoration on door panels and chimneypiece, and with a superbly coloured carpet by Thomas Moore, signed in 1769.

Syon House, on the N bank of the Thames near Brentford, is open daily except Fridays and Saturdays from Good Friday to end September. Tel: 01-560 0881.

△ 2 *Portrait, 1st Duke of Northumberland, 1766.*

▽ 3 *Syon House, Long Gallery, c.1763-8.*

4 *Syon House, Drawing Room, 1762-4.* ▷

KEDLESTON HALL, Derby, Derbyshire

The Viscount Scarsdale

In 1768 Horace Walpole paid a visit to Kedleston. 'The front is heavy' he wrote 'there being no windows, but niches behind the columns'. This south front *(pl.5)* was in Adam's grandest Roman style, and bears a final date of 1765 cut on a panel between the central figures above the entrance. Adam's work at Kedleston — he had been invited by Sir Nathaniel Curzon to take over from the architects Matthew Brettingham and James Paine — can claim to be among the most interesting of his career. The materials are of high quality. Stone was used extensively, and it is significant that the mason's bill (some £6596) was the highest individual amount. Over 55 tons of lead were used on the dome alone. The building of Kedleston summarizes perhaps as completely as any English country house can do the expensive tastes of an owner: the pulling down of a splendid William and Mary house, the construction of a new house in the classical style, and the employment of several architects, with the dominant postion being taken, as on many other occasions, by Robert Adam. He provided interiors of surpassing quality, which Walpole again owned were 'designed by Adam in the best taste'; Dr Johnson and Boswell, however, on their visit found the alabaster pillars in the Marble Hall too 'massy'.

The Dining Room *(pl.6)* and Saloon *(pl.7)* may be regarded as typical of those rooms whose decoration brought together Adam's finest craftsmen, called by Mrs Montagu 'his regiment of artificers'. They it was who gave substance to the architect's careful (often coloured) drawings, and he in turn supervised their execution by choosing able executants, and exercising a complete control over quality of materials, and their fashioning. The Dining Room has ceiling paintings by Antonio Zucchi, one of Adam's favourite painters of decorative ornament, and by William Hamilton and Henry Morland. The latter is credited with the centre panel representing *Love embracing Fortune.* The plasterwork in the apse and on the ceiling is by the successful London firm of plasterers, used almost exclusively by Adam, Joseph Rose & Company. Their detailed bill indicates that they charged £270.3s.3½d for the stucco ornament, which also included the gilded surrounds to the pictures by Zuccarelli, Snyders, Claude and Romanelli. To the left of the apse can be seen (over door) one of William Collins' plaster panels. Collins, who also provided figures for the Marble Hall at Kedleston, specialized in the provision of classical reliefs and sculptures chosen from his extensive catalogue.

The Saloon *(pl.7)* with its coffered dome and niches is the most Roman of Adam's interiors. The paintings of ruins are by William Hamilton, and the grisaille paintings over the niches by Biagio Rebecca.

Kedleston Hall, 4½ miles NW of Derby, is open on Sundays from Easter to September, and on Bank Holiday Mondays and Tuesdays. Tel: 0332 840396.

△ 5 *Kedleston Hall, S front, 1760-5.*

△ 6 *Kedleston Hall, Dining Room, 1760.*

△ 7 *Kedleston Hall, Saloon, 1761-2.*

HAREWOOD HOUSE, Leeds, West Yorkshire

The Earl of Harewood

Harewood House, at first referred to as the 'New House at Gawthorp' was created from 1759 by Edwin Lascelles (1712-95), later Lord Harewood. He used the inheritance bestowed on him by his father, Henry Lascelles, founder and senior partner of a London West India merchant house dealing in sugar and financing loans to planters. After consideration and rejection of plans by William Chambers, and using the Yorkshire architect John Carr to supervise erection of the stables (1755-8), Lascelles turned his attention again to a new house. The competent Carr produced drawings, but after being introduced to Robert Adam, newly returned from Italy, Lascelles asked the ambitious Scotsman to make changes in the drawings. The final solution became a compromise between the plans, with Carr's plan being chosen for the east family apartments and Adam's for the west State Apartments. Harewood House became therefore 'the earliest of Adam's buildings in the pure form of Neo-classicism in domestic architecture'. Work began early in 1759, with the foundation stone being laid by Edwin Lascelles on 23 March. Construction was entrusted to John Carr.

The Long Gallery — a detail of its ceiling is given below *(pl.8)* — was the last room in the house to be completed 'and from its inception has been more subject to alteration than any other'. The first designs for the ceiling are both dated 1765, but three years later Lascelles settled on the present design — a spirited assembly of various shapes, created with dexterity by Joseph Rose & Company; the painted insets are by Biagio Rebecca. The room was 'finished' by the wood pelmets, carved with great skill by Thomas Chippendale to represent taffeta hangings.

Most of the chimneypieces at Harewood were provided by the King's Master Mason, John Devall. The one in the Library, *c.*1769 *(pl.9)* is a fine example of his work, but the overmantel panel, representing a pagan sacrifice (there is a matching chimneypiece on the other side of the room with a panel depicting Bacchic revellers), was provided by William Collins, whose work we have noted at Kedleston *(pl.6)*. The room at Harewood which best demonstrates that particular Adam skill, the blending of the component parts, is the Music Room *(pl.10)*.

Harewood House, 8 miles N of Leeds, is open daily from April to October, and daily except Fridays and Saturdays in February, March and November. Tel: 0532 886225.

▽ 8 *Harewood House, Detail of Long Gallery ceiling, c.1768-9.*

GALLERY

◁ 9 *Harewood House, Library chimneypiece, c.1769.* △ 10 *Harewood House, Music Room, c.1765-71.*

NOSTELL PRIORY, Wakefield, West Yorkshire

The National Trust (gift of Lord St. Oswald, whose home it remains).

As on many other occasions Robert Adam was called upon by Sir Rowland Winn, the builder at Nostell, to add rooms and a wing to an earlier house. In 1733 the Yorkshire amateur architect Colonel James Moyser drew up plans for Nostell, and supervision of the building work was given to the young James Paine (1717-89), who also did much of the detailed designing as the house took shape. The inveterate traveller, Dr Richard Pococke, who saw Nostell in 1750, wrote that it was 'the most convenient I have seen'. However Rowland Winn asked Robert Adam in 1766 to work out the central and northern blocks of the house.

The first room in the house to be remodelled by Adam was the Library *(pl.11)*, the best preserved of the Nostell interiors. The room's unity was achieved by careful juxtaposition of the work of the best craftsmen — paintings by Zucchi, plasterwork by Rose, and furniture by Chippendale. The cabinet-maker's finest and best-documented work is at Nostell, and the superb desk in the foreground *(pl. 7)* was provided by him in 1767 at a cost of £72.10s; it is also shown in the portrait of Sir Rowland and Lady Winn, which stands on an easel near it.

Having completed the Library, Adam moved to the decoration of the Drawing Room (as the Tapestry Room *(pl.12)* was called until the nineteenth century). Zucchi painted the centre of the ceiling with a scene from the story of Cupid and Psyche and lunettes representing the Liberal Arts. His fourteen painted pilasters were removed when Charles Winn acquired the set of Brussels tapestries, *c.*1820.

It may be noted that no Adam interior after the early years was complete without painted decoration. The main artists did on occasion work for architects such as William Chambers and James Wyatt, but their colourful achievements are mainly associated with Robert Adam's designs. The illustrations reproduced in colour in this booklet show the areas which a painter usually filled: the centre, as at Mellerstain *(pl.18)*, and often in addition to this, circles, rectangles, and lozenges like those in the Harewood *(pl.10)* and Nostell *(pl.12)* ceilings.

This process, in the case of Nostell, can be established by reference to the Saloon (*c.*1768-76). In 1773 the ceiling was painted, but Zucchi's paintings, principally of ancient ruins, were still arriving in 1776.

Nostell Priory, 6 miles SE of Wakefield, is open daily from May to September and on Wednesdays, Saturdays and Sundays in April and October. Tel: 0924 863892.

△ 11 *Nostell Priory, Library, 1766-7.*

12 *Nostell Priory, Tapestry Room, 1767.* △

NEWBY HALL, Ripon, North Yorkshire

Mr and Mrs R E J Compton

In 1785 when Robert Adam had finished almost twenty years of involvement with Newby, Lady Bute wrote to Mrs Delany: 'You must have heard of the elegance and magnificence of Mr Weddell's house, all ornamented by Mr Adams, in his highest (and indeed, I think) best taste. There is a gallery fill'd with fine statues, busts and bas-reliefs; a great number of fine pictures dispersed in different rooms; and the drawing-room furnished with the most beautiful Gobelins tapestry I ever saw'. Newby, as Nostell, was an earlier house which had a two-storey wing added by Adam. The main building *(pl. 15)* in red brick was done for Sir William Blackett (d. 1713); Adam was called in by William Weddell (whose father had purchased the estate from John Blackett) to decorate the main rooms and provide a sculpture gallery *(pl.14)*.

Inside, Newby shows most of the decorative elements of the Neo-classical style to advantage on chimneypieces *(pl.16)* and door-cases — the urns, the paterae, the flowing rinceau ornament, and the stylized, enigmatic faces of gods and goddesses, popular with architect and patron alike. Shortly after William Weddell's return from Italy in 1766 with a large collection of sculptures, he commissioned Adam to add a gallery in which to display them. The architect provided designs, some of which are at the house, and arranged the fine room *(pl.14)* as three chambers, the central one domed. The view shows, at left centre, the Barberini *Venus* found in the cellars of the Barberini Palace by Gavin Hamilton. After 'restoration' it was acquired by Weddell with the help of the banker and astute art-dealer Thomas Jenkins.

The Library at Newby *(front cover illus.)* has an apse at each end divided from the centre by wooden columns with Corinthian capitals. At the far end is one of the four alabaster urns mounted on painted pedestals — the other three are elsewhere in the house. Antonio Zucchi painted the ceiling, the central oval depicting the triumph of Bacchus over Ariadne.

As befitted a distinguished connoisseur and patron, one of the five sets of Boucher-Neilson Gobelins tapestries introduced into England was installed at Newby. It is of a different ground colour from the sets made for Croome Court (now in the Metropolitan Museum, New York) and Osterley Park *(pl.23)*. In a shuttered room the colours have stayed brilliant, and captivate the onlooker completely with their *trompe l'oeil* frames, birds, and swags of flowers.

Newby Hall, 4 miles SE of Ripon, is open at certain times from Easter to October. Tel: 09012 2583.

▽ *13 Newby Hall, Staircase Hall, c.1768.*

△ 14 *Newby Hall, Sculpture Gallery, 1767-72.*

△ 15 *Newby Hall, S front (c.1705) with Adam wing, c.1767-76.*

△ 16 *Newby Hall, Detail of Library chimneypiece, c.1770.*

MELLERSTAIN, Gordon, Borders

The Viscount Binning

The castle style which Robert Adam set out in over forty designs was unique to him. The early Adam studies in this genre remained, like many of the remembered wonders of Italian palaces, as impressive drawings only. Ugbrooke in Devon was the first castle of significance, and two in Scotland, Mellerstain and Wedderburn, followed rapidly. At Mellerstain it was a long-held family involvement. On 11 September 1725, the date cut on the foundation plinth of the E wing at Mellerstain, William Adam, Robert's father, inaugurated a great scheme for providing Lady Grisel Baillie with a new house. The centre block, for which drawings exist, was never carried out. Adam built the two wings and for forty years there was nothing between them. At the death of the Earl of Haddington in 1735 his youngest son George succeeded to the Mellerstain estate and assumed the name of Baillie. He it was who employed Robert Adam in 1770 to design the centre portion of the house *(pl.17)*. After thoughts of Gothicizing it he merely added battlements and hood moulds over the windows. It was a dull solution, but all his attention was lavished on the splendid interior.

The Library *(pl.18)*, with its four long stucco panels and busts by Scheemakers and Roubiliac in the niches, may be counted as among the very finest work of Adam's mature period. The detail in the room — in chimneypiece, pelmets, bookcases, and frieze — adds up, as Mark Girouard has noted 'to an effect of perfection'. The stucco panels were based on those on the tomb of the Roman Emperor Severus at Monte del Grano, copied from a 1727 book of engravings by Santo Bartoli. The panels are surmounted by a delicate palmette and anthemia frieze. Adam's design for the ceiling is dated 5 March 1778. It may be assumed that painted roundels such as those at its centre were still provided for Scottish houses by experienced painters such as Zucchi. In oil on paper or on canvas it would be a comparatively simple task to provide them from London, done to a measured drawing.

The plasterers Adam used in Scotland are less well known than his usual London firm of Joseph Rose & Company. It would seem that Thomas Clayton junior was a favourite; in addition, a number of plasterers who worked at Inveraray Castle would have been capable of fashioning the Mellerstain ceilings. That of the Dining (now Music) Room *(pl.19)* follows an Adam drawing dated 7 September 1773. The centre medallion is surrounded by an octagon of flowing rinceau and fan ornament, with eagles and medallions at the four corners.

Mellerstain, 37 miles SE of Edinburgh, is open daily except Saturdays from May to September. Tel: 057381 225.

△ 17 *Mellerstain, S front from terrace, c.1770.*

18 *See pp: 16-17* *Mellerstain, Library, 1770-1* ▷

△ 19 *Mellerstain, Ceiling of Dining (now Music) Room, 1773.*

KENWOOD, Hampstead, London

Greater London Council (The Iveagh Bequest)

Kenwood was built by Robert Adam for the distinguished judge, William Murray, 1st Earl of Mansfield, in the comparatively short space of two years, 1767-8. In describing work of which he was proud, justifiably so, Robert Adam wrote of the Library, his finest room *(pl.21)* in his *Works in Architecture* (1773-8) : 'whatever defects, either in beauty or composition, shall be discovered in the following designs, they must be imputed to me alone'. As a fellow Scot it was natural that Lord Mansfield should turn to Adam, now one of the most celebrated architects of his day. He was to support him further when, as Lord Chief Justice, he acted in favour of the architect in the Liardet patent stucco case (1778). This allowed Adam to tighten his hold on the market for providing panels, bas-reliefs and other ornaments in composition stucco.

At Kenwood Adam added a storey to the main block of the house and, observing symmetry, added the Library on the E side to balance the Orangery. The Library was also intended by him to act as a room for receiving company. It was given circular recesses for the books, and the body of the room was 'made suitable for the latter'. With gilded plaster decorations by Joseph Rose junior, paintings (1769) by Antonio Zucchi, and furniture from Thomas Chippendale and William France, Lord Mansfield had every reason to be satisfied with the outcome. The architect took delight in the ancient classical form of the barrel vault ceiling, delicately coloured 'to take off the glare of white', and with Zucchi's inset paintings, the centre roundel depicting *The Choice of Hercules.* The plasterwork was, as usual, by Joseph Rose & Company, and the wood carvers, John Minshull and Saffron Nelson enriched the window shutters, the soffits of the windows, the doors, bookcases, pilasters and the frame of David Martin's portrait of Lord Mansfield above the chimneypiece.

The portico on the N front *(pl.20)* with its composite columns remains also almost as Adam designed it. The wings at each side were added by George Saunders, a follower of the architect Henry Holland in 1793-6. In July 1770, Lady Mary Coke, who had just dined at Kenwood, wrote to a friend: 'The improvements since I saw it are very great; Lord Mansfield has laid out a vast deal of money and with a very good taste. The great room he has built is as fine as it can possibly be; no expense spared'.

Kenwood, in NW London, is open daily except Good Friday, Christmas Eve and Christmas Day. Tel: 01-348 1286.

△ 20 *Kenwood, Portico on N Front, c.1769-70.*

△ 21 *Kenwood, Library, 1767-9.*

OSTERLEY PARK, Hounslow, London

The National Trust (Administered by the Victoria & Albert Museum)

Built originally in 1577 by Sir Thomas Gresham, Osterley is one of the many houses completely remodelled to the highest standards by Robert Adam. His work there spanned most of his active career, from 1761 until 1780. The adherence to classical forms starts with the Great Portico *(pl.22)* *c.*1762, which connects the two wings of the N front. Horace Walpole, a frequent visitor to the house, wrote to the Countess of Upper Ossory on 21 June 1773: 'there is a double portico that fills the space between the towers of the front and is as noble as the Propylaeum of Athens'. The important influence on the design of the Osterley portico — apart from allusions to that of the Temple of the Sun at Palmyra — was William Talman's work in the early 18th century at Witham Park, Somerset which Robert Adam visited in connection with work he was doing there in 1762. Work at Osterley was for Francis Child, a London banker, and after his death in 1763, for his brother, Robert Child .

The Entrance Hall *(pl.24)*, 1767-8, shows the successful synthesis of the flat and linear motifs, now common in Adam's maturing style. There is a careful pattern relationship between ceiling and inlaid floor, the focal points of apse and wall panels, and the delicate blue and white colouring. The Roman-inspired trophies, based on those on the Campidoglio in Rome — the Trophies of Marius — were used at both Syon (Ante-Room) and at Osterley, and executed in plaster composition by the faithful Joseph Rose & Company.

The beautiful Library *(pl.25)* at Osterley was designed in 1766, and after much amendment was complete by 1773. The inset paintings are by Zucchi, and the house, fortunate to retain so much of its original furniture, provides the setting here for desk and chairs by John Linnell (1770) and bookcases (almost certainly) by John Gilbert, whose name appears regularly in Adams's bank account from the opening entry in 1764.

Walpole visited Osterley again in 1778. He described the Tapestry Room *(pl.23)* as 'the most superb and beautiful that can be imagined', but at the same time he blamed Adam for 'sticking diminutive heads in bronze, no bigger than half a crown, into the chimneypiece's hair'.

Osterley Park, in West London, is open daily except Mondays, but is also open on Bank Holiday Mondays. Tel: 01-560 3918.

△ 22 *Osterley Park, View from inner courtyard through portico.*

△ *23 Osterley Park. Tapestry Room, c.1773.*

△ 24 *Osterley Park, Entrance Hall, 1767-8.*
▽ 25 *Osterley Park, Library, 1766-73.*

CULZEAN CASTLE, Maybole, Strathclyde
The National Trust for Scotland

In the late 17th century Culzean was described as 'standing on a rock above the sea, flanged upon the south with very pretty gardens and orchards ...so well sheltered from the north and east winds...'. A hundred years later additions were made to this fortified tower for the 9th Earl of Cassillis. In 1777 the 10th Earl, his brother, asked Robert Adam to reconstruct the interior and add the wings facing over the extensive terraced gardens. Adam continued to add to the turreted house until his death in 1792, and in the Victorian period, the 3rd Marquess of Ailsa added a west wing, more terraced gardens and a famous collection of trees and shrubs which thrive in the mild Gulf Stream climate.

Culzean, the most spectacular of Robert Adam's castle houses, was sited dramatically *(pls. 27, 30)* on a rocky site above the Irish Sea. With its four round towers and the higher central section incorporating the 16th century tower-house Culzean owes a stylistic debt to Wedderburn Castle, Borders (1770-8), which Adam designed for Patrick Home. Adam had it in mind from the early 1760s to design an oval staircase, and he achieved the aim finally with great distinction at Culzean. He had proposed one at Great Saxham, Suffolk, for Hutchinson Mure (1779), but his second plans for rebuilding after the fire there were not accepted. He proposed another in an (unexecuted) design of 1789 at Cullen House, Grampian, for the Earl of Findlater. But that at Culzean *(pl.28)* stands supreme, rising on two tiers of twelve columns (with Corintian and Ionic capitals respectively) to an oval dome.

Another beautiful interior at Culzean is the Round Drawing Room *(pl.29) c.*1790. The disposing of doors and windows and the setting-out of a ceiling in a circular room brought out the best in Adam's craftsmen. The ceiling drawings at the Soane Museum do not refer to this room, but the one at Culzean of 1790 is as executed. The carpet was also made for the room. The anonymous author of *A Tour...to the Western Highlands of Scotland* (1788) wrote: 'his Lordship, not content with the present extensive pile, intends adding a similar front to the sea, which will be a most arduous undertaking from the vast depth of the foundation necessary to be formed. At present it does great credit to Adam, the architect, and his Lordship's peculiar taste and will, when complete, stand unrivalled in its way'.

Culzean Castle, 12 miles SW of Ayr, is open daily from April to October. Tel: 06556 269.

◁ 26 *Osterley Park, Etruscan Dressing Room, c.1775-6.*

27 *Culzean Castle, N front, from the shore, c.1790.* ▽

△ 28 *Culzean Castle. Oval Staircase, c.1790.*
29 *Culzean Castle, Round Drawing Room, c.1790.* ▷

△ 30 *Culzean Castle. Drawing of S front, c.1786.*

31 Saltram House, Saloon, 1768-9. ▷

SALTRAM HOUSE, Plymouth, Devon
The National Trust

Where the river Plym broadens into its estuary stands Saltram, the largest country house in Devon. The traveller and writer William Gilpin in his *Observations on the Western parts of England* (1798) likened it to 'Mount Edgcomb in miniature, being situated in a small peninsula, and surrounded, not indeed by the sea, but by a considerable creek'. After John Parker's marriage in 1725 he added to the old house at Saltram, including work by an unknown Italian stuccoist. It was his eldest son, also John Parker, who succeeded in 1768 and who invited Adam to decorate the two principal rooms of Saloon and Dining Room.

The Saloon, or as it was called in the Saltram accounts, 'The Great Room', is one of the noblest proportions *(pl.31),* intended for formal receptions and social occasions. Furniture was usually ranged around the walls and extra prominence was thus accorded by both the designer and his eventual audience to the ceiling and the carpet. Saltram is fortunate to retain its original carpet, delivered from Thomas Whitty of Axminster in 1770 at a charge of £126. John Parker and his Yorkshire wife, Theresa Robinson, took the keenest interest in the decoration of their home. Reynolds' admiration and affection for her is revealed in his description of her after her death, and his great canvas of her is among the finest of his several works at Saltram.

What the Parkers were able to give Adam therefore, was a sympathetic and caring concern for his considerable decorative achievements. They patronized Thomas Chippendale for furniture, obtained ormolu *torchères* from Matthew Boulton (1772), table frames from Joseph Perfetti, tables from Henry Kettle, and collected bronzes, pictures and the *objets d'arts*.

The furnishing and decoration of the Dining Room *(back cover illus)* took place in two stages. In 1768 Adam submitted a design which included wall and ceiling painting positions for Antonio Zucchi to paint. The second stage came about 1780 when John Parker (now Viscount Boringdon) decided to change the positions of his library and eating room. Adam may have supervised the work, but in any case Zucchi was asked to fill in the spaces left by the removal of bookcases with large paintings of the kind the artist had provided at Harewood *(pl.10).* The chimneypiece designed in 1768 was probably supplied by Thomas Carter the Younger of Piccadilly who worked for Adam at Syon and elsewhere. The dining-table is not original to Saltram, and in any case Adam did not intend there to be a centrally placed table. We do not know whether he designed the carpet, but as it matches the ceiling patterns, and was provided by Whitty, there is every reason to assume he did do so.

Saltram House, 3½ miles E of Plymouth, is open daily except Mondays from April to October. Tel: 0752 336546.

Triangles in red signify works of Robert Adam mentioned in this book.
Triangles in black signify other buildings to which Robert Adam contributed.
Names of Robert Adam's works are listed by number (*see* p.31) to correspond with those shown on the map
County boundaries
Towns/Cities
0 20 40 60 75 miles
0 40 80 120 kilometres
HIGHLAND
GRAMPIAN
TAYSIDE
CENTRAL
FIFE
LOTHIAN
STRATHCLYDE
BORDERS
DUMFRIES & GALLOWAY
NORTHUMBERLAND
TYNE & WEAR
DURHAM
CLEVELAND
CUMBRIA
NORTH YORKSHIRE
LANCASHIRE
W. YORKSHIRE
HUMBERSIDE
MERSEYSIDE
GREATER MANCHESTER
SOUTH YORKSHIRE
CHESHIRE
DERBYSHIRE
NOTTS.
LINCOLNSHIRE
CLWYD
GWYNEDD
STAFFORDSHIRE
SHROPSHIRE
LEICESTERSHIRE
WEST MIDLANDS
NORFOLK
CAMBS.
NORTHANTS
WARKS.
POWYS
HEREFORD & WORCESTER
DYFED
SUFFOLK
BEDS.
BUCKS.
HERTS.
ESSEX
GLOUCESTERSHIRE
OXFORDSHIRE
WEST GLAM.
MID GLAM.
GWENT
STH. GLAM.
GRT. LONDON
AVON
WILTSHIRE
BERKSHIRE
SURREY
KENT
SOMERSET
HAMPSHIRE
WEST SUSSEX
EAST SUSSEX
DEVON
DORSET
CORNWALL
ISLE OF WIGHT
ISLE OF MAN
NORTHERN IRELAND
EIRE
IRISH SEA
NORTH SEA
ENGLISH CHANNEL
Inverness
Nairn
Aberdeen
Dundee
Perth
Dunfermline
Edinburgh
Glasgow
Galashiels
Ayr
Dumfries
Alnwick
Belfast
Dublin
York
Leeds
Manchester
Liverpool
Sheffield
Derby
King's Lynn
Norwich
Birmingham
Huntingdon
Bury St Edmunds
Warwick
Northampton
Cambridge
Worcester
Ipswich
Hereford
Buckingham
Colchester
Luton
Hertford
Chelmsford
Bristol
Cardiff
Bath
Maidstone
Canterbury
Guildford
Hastings
Exeter
Plymouth
Truro
1
2
3
4
5
6-10
11
12
13
14
15-17
18
19
20
21
22
23
24-25
26-7
28
29
30
31
32-33
34
35
36
37
38
39-40
41
42
43
44
45
46
47
48
49
50
51
52
53
54-72
69
70
71
73
74
75
76
77
78
79
80
81

THE WORKS OF ROBERT ADAM

The map and the key (*see* p. 30) indicate those buildings and monuments that survive as examples of Adam's work at the time of writing. Counties named in the key are those that existed before local government reorganization (1974 and 1975). The relation of the buildings and monuments listed below to the new counties can be seen by reference to the map.

1 **FORT GEORGE**, Inverness-shire, 1752.
2 **PITFOUR CASTLE**, Perthshire, *c.* 1790.
3 **COUNTY HOUSE**, Kinross, 1771.
4 **HOPETOUN HOUSE**, West Lothian, 1751-.
5 **NEWLISTON**, West Lothian, 1790-2.
6 **THE GENERAL REGISTER HOUSE**, Edinburgh, 1774-92.
7 **THE UNIVERSITY**, Edinburgh, 1789-91.
8 **CHARLOTTE SQUARE**, Edinburgh, 1791-1807.
9 **7 QUEEN STREET** (now Royal College of Physicians), Edinburgh, 1770-1.
10 **Monument to DAVID HUME** (d.1776), erected 1778, Old Calton churchyard, Edinburgh.
11 **BRIDGE**, Dalkeith, Midlothian, 1792.
12 **OXENFOORD CASTLE**, Midlothian, 1780-2.
13 **GOSFORD HOUSE**, Longniddry, East Lothian, 1792-1803.
14 **DUNBAR HOUSE**, East Lothian, 1790-2.
15 **ASSEMBLY ROOMS**, Glasgow, 1796-8.
16 **POLLOK HOUSE**, Glasgow, 1752.
17 **TRADES HALL**, Glasgow, 1791-9.
18 **WEDDERBURN CASTLE**, Berwickshire, 1770.
19 **MELLERSTAIN**, Berwickshire, 1770-8.
20 **AUCHINCRUIVE**, Ayrshire. Garden tower, 1778.
21 **CULZEAN CASTLE**, Ayrshire, 1777-90.
22 **KIRKOSWALD CHURCH**, Ayrshire, 1777.
23 **DALQUHARRAN CASTLE**, Girvan, Ayrshire, 1785, (ruined).
24 **DUMFRIES HOUSE**, Ayrshire, 1754-9.
25 **Column to memory of DUKE OF QUEENSBERRY**, erected 1780, Market Place, Dumfries.
26 **BRISLEE TOWER**, Alnwick, Northumberland. Gothic folly, *c.* 1778-9.
27 **HULNE PRIORY**, Alnwick, Northumberland, Gothic interiors, *c.* 1778.
28 **NEWBY HALL**, Ripon, Yorkshire, Porch wings, interiors, 1767-80.
29 **HAREWOOD HOUSE**, Yorkshire, 1759-71.
30 **BYRAM HALL**, Yorkshire. Library and other interiors, 1780.
31 **NOSTELL PRIORY**, Wakefield, Yorkshire. Added wing, stables, interiors, 1766-70.
32 **KEDLESTON HOUSE**, Derbyshire, South front, interiors, 1760-70.
33 **Monument to SIR NATHANIEL CURZON (d.1758)**, Kedleston church, Derbyshire.
34 **GUNTON CHURCH** Norfolk, 1769.
35 **KIMBOLTON CASTLE**, Huntingdonshire. Gatehouse and entrance screen, 1765.
36 **Monument to MARY, 3rd DUCHESS OF MONTAGU (d.1771)**, Warkton church, Northamptonshire.
37 **COMPTON VERNEY**, Warwickshire, Wings, interiors, orangery, bridge, 1761-5.
38 **Monument to BISHOP JAMES JOHNSON (d.1774)**, Worcester Cathedral.
39 **CROOME COURT**, Croome d'Abitot, Worcestershire, Interiors, certain garden buildings, 1760-80.
40 **CROOME CHURCH**, Worcestershire. Fittings, 1763.
41 **MOCCAS COURT**, Herefordshire, 1775-81.
42 **THEATRE AND MARKET HALL** (Now Town Hall), Bury St Edmunds, Suffolk, 1775-80.
43 **AUDLEY END**, Essex. Interiors, 1762-5.
44 **MISTLEY CHURCH** Essex, 1776, dem. except for towers.
45 **WEALD HALL**, Essex, Interiors, 1778.
46 **HITCHIN PRIORY**, Hertfordshire, South front, 1777.
47 **WORMLEYBURY**, Hertfordshire. Interiors, 1777-9.
48 **STOWE**, Buckinghamshire. Garden front, portico, 1771-.
49 **SHARDELOES**, Buckinghamshire. Portico, interiors, stables. 1759-61.
50 **SHAMBLES AND BUTTER MARKET**, High Wycombe, Buckinghamshire, 1761.
51 **WEST WYCOMBE PARK**, Buckinghamshire. Kitchen and stable wing, 1767-8.
52 **PULTENEY BRIDGE**, Bath, Somerset, 1769-74.
53 **BOWOOD HOUSE**, Wiltshire, Portico, interiors, 1761-4; mausoleum, 1763.
54 **LONDON, ADELPHI**, begun 1772, dem. except 7 ADAM STREET, ceiling of 6 ROYAL TERRACE, re-erected, Victoria & Albert Museum.
55 **LONDON, ADMIRALTY**, Screen Wall, 1760.
56 **ASHBURNHAM HOUSE**, (now No 30), Dover Street, London, 1773-6.
57 **LANSDOWNE HOUSE**, Berkeley Square, London, 1762. Drawing Room re-created at Philadelphia Museum of Art; Dining Room at Metropolitan Museum, New York.
58 **CHANDOS HOUSE**, Chandos Street, London, 1770.
59 **30 CURZON STREET**, London, 1771.
60 **FITZROY SQUARE**, London, 1790-1800. South and east sides.
61 **MANSFIELD STREET**, London, 1770-5.
62 **NORTHUMBERLAND HOUSE**, London, 1770; dem. 1874. Glass Drawing Room re-erected, Victoria & Albert Museum.
63 **106 PICCADILLY**, London. Interiors, 1765-6.
64 **20 PORTMAN SQUARE** London (Home House), 1775-7.
65 **ROYAL SOCIETY OF ARTS**, John Street, London, 1772-4.
66 **20 ST JAMES'S SQUARE**, London, 1772-4.
67 **29 SACKVILLE STREET** London. Ceiling, 1770.
68 **Westminster Abbey**, London: monuments to MAJOR JOHN ANDRÉ (d.1780), MARY HOPE (d.1767), ELIZABETH, DUCHESS OF NORTHUMBERLAND (d.1776), JAMES THOMSON (d.1748), LT-COL. ROGER TOWNSHEND (d.1759).
69 **KENWOOD**, Hampstead, Middlesex, Library, portico, 1767-9.
70 **OSTERLEY HOUSE**, Middlesex, 1761-80.
71 **SYON HOUSE**, Middlesex. Remodelled interior, 1762-9, entrance screen, 1773.
72 **Monument to ROBERT CHILD (d.1782)**, Heston church, Middlesex.
73 **HATCHLANDS**, Surrey, Interiors, 1758-61.
74 **BRASTED HOUSE**, Kent, 1784-5.
75 **MERSHAM LE HATCH**, Kent. House and interiors, 1762-5.
76 **ASHBURNHAM, PLACE**, Sussex. Entrance lodges, 1785.
77 **UGBROOKE PARK**, Devon. South and west fronts, 1764-8, and some interior work, 1766-71.
78 **SALTRAM HOUSE**, Devon. Interior decorations, 1768-9.
79 **Monument to ADMIRAL, THE HON EDWARD BOSCAWEN (d.1761)**, church (St Michael) at St Michael Penkevil, Cornwall.

80 **CASTLE UPTON**, Co. Antrim, Ireland. Additions, 1788.
81 **HEADFORT**, Co. Meath, Ireland, 1770. Designed by Adam but erected with some alterations to his plans and under other supervision.